On the
Teaching and
Writing of History

BERNARD BAILYN

On the Teaching and Writing of History

Responses to a series of questions

Edited by
Edward Connery Lathem

HANOVER · NEW HAMPSHIRE
Montgomery Endowment
Dartmouth College

DISTRIBUTED BY
University Press of New England

Kenneth and Harle Montgomery Endowment
Dartmouth College, Hanover, New Hampshire

This presentation of informal responses to a series of questions relating to the teaching and
writing of history is based upon and extends
from two tape-recorded "Conversations" that
were engaged in by Bernard Bailyn with Pro-
fessors Jere R. Daniell and Charles T. Wood of
the Dartmouth College Department of History,
during Professor Bailyn's period in residence as
Montgomery Fellow at Dartmouth in 1991.

ISBN 0–87451–712–5 (cloth)
ISBN 0–87451–720–6 (paper)

Frontispiece: Bernard Bailyn at Dartmouth in
1991, by John Douglas/Flying Squirrel Graphics

Distribution: University Press of New England
Hanover, New Hampshire 03755

On the
Teaching and
Writing of History

To begin quite basically, Professor Bailyn, how would you define "history"?

🕉 B.B. 🕉 The word "history" has, I think, two meanings. One is simply *what happened*; that is, the events, developments, circumstances, and thoughts of the past, as they actually occurred. The other is history as *knowledge of what happened*, the record or expression of what occurred.

Carl Becker, a leading historian a generation or so ago, gave as good a definition of history—in the second of these two senses, *knowledge of the past*—as I know of. History, he said in an address to the American Historical Association in 1931, is simply "the memory of things said and done." And it functions, he added, as "the artificial extension of the social memory."

"The memory of things said and done" does not pretend to be the recall of all past experience. It is a necessarily imperfect and selective reconstruction. But it serves to extend and to enlarge our own, personal experience and to orient contemporary issues, values, goals, and behavior.

One needs to understand the relationship between the reality of what happened—the totality of past events

and developments, past circumstances and thoughts—
and what, in historical writings and compilations, people represent them to have been. That relationship, it
seems to me, is crucial to all historical study and knowledge. The accuracy and adequacy of representations of
past actualities, the verisimilitude or closeness to fact of
what is written about them, remain the measure, in the
end, of good history—this despite all the fashionable
doubts that are raised about the attainment of absolute or
perfect objectivity and accuracy (which no one pretends
to, anyway).

And how would you describe or characterize what a
"historian" is?

❧ B.B. ❦ A historian, I assume, is someone who de-
velops, in one way or another, what Becker called the
"artificial extension of social memory"—by recovering,
through the evidences of the past, aspects of what happened. But that does not confine historians to people
who teach in colleges and universities. One of the interesting things about the practice of history these days is
that history, while largely the domain of academicians, is
not entirely so.

First of all, you have some well-known historians
who are non-academicians, yet people who are professionally trained. Barbara Tuchman was a prime example.
She had the credentials of a professional scholar, even

though she practiced, so to speak, as an amateur—in the sense that she was not involved in the critical, systematic development of knowledge in certain areas and was not responsible for passing on to the next generation a large-scale, integrated picture of what our past has been.

Then, too, there are more and more "public historians"; that is, professionally trained historians who do not teach in universities or who do not write as Barbara Tuchman did, but who work in commercial organizations that provide accurate historical studies, on a contract basis. For example, there is the Winthrop Group, in Cambridge, Massachusetts, a team of excellent historians who run a commercial organization that serves a variety of historical functions. They work for business corporations that want company histories written or that want their archives put in order or want an accurate historical record kept of an on-going experimental project. They also do historical research for legal briefs, where objective history by impartial scholars can be critical, and they arrange for oral histories.

Third, another group of non-academic historians work in state, regional, and local historical societies, museums, and restorations. They are experts in regional history or masters of specific archives for which they provide valuable guides and from which they publish documentary series. Often they are involved in or help sponsor the editing of the new "Papers" series. Julian Boyd, the first editor of the great *Papers of Thomas Jeffer-*

son series, set a standard for technical scholarship in such editing, beyond anything known before in this country, and he established a new style for what are, in effect, massive documentary biographies. His volumes—like the new Adams, Madison, Washington, and other "Papers," all of them works of excellent historical scholarship—provide basic source material that historians of all kinds will use for generations to come.

It is amusing to contrast Boyd, a meticulous scholar who reproduced every orthographic peculiarity of the original texts and published variant readings of every word that was not perfectly clear in the original, with predecessors like Jared Sparks, the nineteenth-century President of Harvard, who falsified the texts of Washington's letters, because he thought they were too colloquial—even, indelicate.

Finally, there are historians who are professional journalists. Theodore White, famous for his presidential-campaign histories, established his reputation as a journalist covering China, whose history he had studied extensively with John Fairbank at Harvard; he prided himself on his writing on the history of modern China. Journalists like White or like Theodore Draper (his book on the Iran-Contra affair, *A Very Thin Line*, is a first-class work of history) are important figures in the historical world. They write contemporary history—which has both positive and negative sides. On the one hand, they capture the immediacy of a situation, because they are almost participants or can talk to the actual participants. What they write has a vividness that no historian dealing with the deeper past can have. On the other hand, they lack the perspective that a historian reaching back a hundred years would have. Their perspective is necessarily shallow. They don't know, cannot know, all of the circumstances, nor what the eventualities will be—and so, in the end, the costs. But they certainly do convey, as I say, the vividness of events, the peculiar atmospheres and moods and the complex balances of personalities that only participants can truly grasp.

This kind of history attracts some of the best academic historians, too. Arthur Schlesinger Jr. wrote a biography of John Kennedy very soon after the President was assassinated, and since he was a member of the White House staff and knew Kennedy well and admired him, his book, while partisan, has a wonderful immediacy and a sense of the personalities involved that no later historian would be able to capture. But inevitably—necessarily—there was much that he did not know, could not have known, about Kennedy and about the circumstances that shaped his life and brief presidency.

But the preponderance of historical writing does, of course, come from universities.

Why should one study history?

ⓒ B.B. ⓢ That seems to divide into two questions:

why history should be studied, and why I—or you or any other individual—should study it in any but the way a normally well-informed person would.

History should be studied because it is an absolutely necessary enlargement of human experience, a way of getting out of the boundaries of one's own life and culture and of seeing more of what human experience has been. And it is the necessary, unique way of orienting the present moment, so that you know where you are and where we have come from and so you don't fantasize about the past and make up myths to justify some immediate purpose—so you can make decisions based to some extent on what has gone before, on knowledge of actual experience.

Accurate historical knowledge is essential for social sanity. Pathological systems—totalitarian regimes of whatever kind, of the left or the right—must systematically distort history in order to survive. Goebbels knew that; Stalin and his lackeys in the Soviet Writers' Guild knew that. So did George Orwell when he assigned the hero of *1984* the task of falsifying the past. Society's need for history, as complete and objective as possible, is obvious.

Why anyone in particular should study history is a different question. My answer to that is that you should study it—beyond what any informed person should know—if it interests you. Somebody's got to study it thoroughly and systematically if our society is to keep its sanity, its sense of reality and self-awareness, but I think the individuals who study history professionally should do so because it attracts them, because it satisfies them intellectually. If it doesn't interest one, there are many other things to devote oneself to.

History is taught in our schools at every level, from the primary grades onward. What is there to be said, in a general way, about differences of approach to instruction at the various learning levels?

☾ B.B. ☽ I have taught at two levels: at the graduate level and in courses for undergraduates. I find the graduate level of teaching not at all difficult, and I don't prepare much for it. Graduate students are beginning to do what I am doing. The task is to show them techniques and to create taste and control over the material; to make them aware that there are good, useful, and important questions and that there are trivial questions; to lead them to understand the difference and to know what significance is.

Beyond that, the task is to sensitize graduate students' minds to all sorts of creative possibilities. I try to do this by any means I can find. I have, for example, asked graduate students to read clusters of writings on what would appear to be unified topics—like, say, the history of education: four books on the history of education. But what I really intended them to focus on and learn about had nothing to do with the history of education. It was something entirely different—perhaps narrative structure or literary style or how *not* to frame a problem. I don't tell them this in advance. So, at first, in the discussion they are a little confused. The next time, they don't know what to expect. And at the end of a number of weeks of this, their minds are open to all sorts of issues, and they read in several dimensions simultaneously. That seems to be a way of sensitizing them to various possibilities of explanation and interpretation, and a way also of conveying a sense of taste and style.

All that is a very different thing from undergraduate teaching, which is an effort to convey the structure of an entire subject, rather than an approach to historical study. One's obligation is to present, at an elementary level, a whole subject in an integrated form for intelligent, critical, but uninformed people. That means boiling down a great deal of technical material into a general story and presenting it as a whole, so that when the course is over, the student really can see the outline of the overall subject. It takes a great deal of effort to fuse into a single coherent account all the details, all the information available. One has to presume no knowledge on the part of the students and has to provide both structure and sufficient detail for the story as a whole. That is not easy to do—at least in an original way.

But is there not a high degree of repetition in undergraduate instruction; and, accordingly, ought not in-

struction at that level to be increasingly less time-consuming, year after year?

☉ B.B. ☉ There is no question but that the first round in a new undergraduate course takes a tremendous amount of work, if one is to present the subject properly. Thereafter, one is dealing with refinements and qualifications, shifts and changes. But I have never given a course—even when it is a familiar one—in which I haven't worked through all the material again, checking back, knowing that between the time I last gave it and the time I am now giving it, any number of new things have come out on the subject, and that my own approach may have shifted, due to other work I was doing and my own second thoughts.

The tough thing in teaching undergraduates—for me, anyway—has been to pull together all this technical material and all the products of new technologies, into a coherent story and at the same time explore the problems of interpretation. It is hard to cover all the material, old and new, and to make it intelligible for people who are not professionally engaged in historical study. The graduate students are committed; they are doing, as I say, the same kind of thing I am doing, and they want me to help them get on with their own work. But the undergraduates make greater demands, because the technical work has to be put into intelligible form for them.

What does "intelligible" mean in that context? It seems to be something different from what it means with respect to graduate students.

❦ B.B. ❧ I think it *is* different, and I think the same question of intelligibility applies when you write for a general reader and not for technicians in the field. What do you concentrate on in teaching undergraduates or in writing for general readers? What issues should you isolate for analysis and description? The answer, for me, is that the framing issues should be those that contribute to an understanding of some critical phase in the process by which a distant and different past moved toward our familiar present. But these critical transitions have to be analyzed without any sense of inevitability or necessary progress; they have to be seen in all their complexity and with all the accidental, contingent elements highlighted —and, as I say, with no assumption that change means progress or that purpose determines outcome.

This very general idea has shaped much of my own work in history. That is the fascination, to me, of early modern history: the long era of transition to modernity—far enough away to provide a deep perspective on the present and to isolate critical turning points, yet close enough to modernity for one to recognize elements of a familiar world in their original form. Understanding early modern history gives one a purchase on understanding the modern world, which one otherwise would not have. At the same time, in both teaching and writing, I have tried to link America and the rest of the world, because that connection also helps explain our lives. And I have tried, too, in various ways to link intellectual developments with social and political developments. All of this, I believe, helps explain how we got where we are. And that, in the largest sense, is what history should do for the general reader and for the beginning student.

What about history teaching at the high-school level?

⊙ B.B. ⊙ Anything I say about this has to be qualified by the fact that I've never taught in a high school. But, for what it is worth, let me say that there seem to me to be two rather contradictory obligations in high-school teaching, both of which are very important.

In the first place, because young people can memorize easily, it is a time in which one can give them basic structural lines to large-scale historical narratives—basic information, so they know that there was an English Civil War, that Rome follows the great era of Ancient Greece, that neither Germany nor Italy was a nation until the nineteenth century, that Napoleon follows the French Revolution and that what he did was related to it, et cetera—so that they get the grid lines of large areas of history, within which later details can be fitted. But that can be a very routine, mechanical, and rather boring business that students are not attracted to, unless taught by an exceptionally engaging teacher. One way of handling this, it seems to me, is to convey information in terms of questions that are not contrived—real questions that might appeal to students' natural curiosity.

I recently had a conversation with people at the Harvard Graduate School of Education who were concerned about this problem. They were preparing a section for a school curriculum on the Bill of Rights, and they asked me how I would present this if I were teaching in a high school. I said that one of the interesting things about the federal Bill of Rights is that it is so different from the bills of rights of the individual states. The prescriptive verbs in the states' bills of rights are "ought"s, and they are cast in terms of general philosophical principles. For example, "All men ought to be free." But the United States Bill of Rights is a mandate on Congress, and the operative verbs are different. It says, "Congress shall not. . . ." The language is mandatory, not optative—and not by accident.

That seems to me to pose a real problem of explanation. Why the difference? I believe if you put it to bright high-school students they will see that it's a question that really requires an answer, and they will want to find an answer. If one can go through major topics in terms of real questions of that kind—interpretative questions—I think you can engage the students.

Carl Becker, whom I mentioned before, wrote a

high-school textbook framed by paradoxes or provoca-
tive topic headings: "How the French people started out
to make a small revolution and ended by making a great
one"; "Why the members of the Third Estate took a
long time deciding whether they should sit in three
rooms or in one"; "How the Jacobins, after having saved
the revolution, destroyed themselves"; "Was Napoleon
a great man?" The worst thing, it seems to me, is simply
to dish out descriptive history without offering questions, some general ideas, a framework to hang it on.
You have to have some kind of hook for the information, or it's just brute force and nobody will, in the end,
respond positively to that.

The second thing that I assume is important to do at
this stage is simply to fascinate high-school students with
history—get them excited about it, show the fascination
of events, personalities, and outcomes; emphasize the
drama and personal interest of it all—so they see that this
is something that can be vitally, intrinsically interesting
to them, and not something dull.

These two things—imparting to students substantial
amounts of basic historical information and at the same
time developing in them a genuine interest in history—
might seem to run against each other. The ideal of high-
school teaching is to do both, and I hope there are high-
school teachers who can do this. The great obligation
at this level is to see to it that students don't come into
college-level study or into their own independent read-

ing of history without any kind of structural lines to the larger story. They must have something to hang the later information on, and they must at the same time take with them from high school some sense that it is enjoyable to study history.

How does one best approach the necessary task of examining individuals on what they have learned during their study of history?

⚙ B.B. ☯ People have different views about this. My feeling, first of all, is that examinations should not focus on historians. I don't think historians, with a few exceptions, are very important. *History* is important. So, I don't want to stick a student with deciding in an exam between differences in the interpretations of Historian A and Historian B. I don't think they should be adjudicating between historians huddled over their desks trying to write books, or concentrating on how one historian's interpretation differs from another's.

For me a good test requires a student to mobilize the information learned, in order to deal with fresh questions about the substance of history that he or she hasn't thought of before, but which can be answered with the materials studied. That forces one to break out of a given formulation and to use the data in a fresh way. Sometimes it's difficult to pose an interesting question that will require the student to reorganize and rethink the information available, direct it to questions not considered before, and write up coherent answers. But that kind of exam seems to me to be worth the trouble.

What about textbooks in history?

❦ B.B. ❧ I think of this generally in terms of the contrast between English and American textbooks. English textbooks—that is, general introductory surveys—are often hard for Americans to use, because they frequently turn out to be extended essays of interpretation, written with the assumption that the student has at least the bare outline of the story to begin with. (That presumes something about English secondary-school education that is, by the way, less and less true these days. In any case, that is what is assumed; namely, that the outline was gained in secondary school.) Therefore, the English textbook writers are really essayists, interpreters, and commentators. They take it for granted that you know something about Wolsey or whomever, and they comment on and interpret his career. But the American student, who doesn't know Wolsey from Cranmer, can be quite bewildered by this.

American textbooks are much more descriptive of basic information. The difficulty for us is to make the text an interesting book, despite the necessity of delivering elementary information that a student who knows nothing will need. Yet, in trying to make it an engaging and readable book one cannot revert to the essay form—largely interpretation and commentary.

I have been involved in textbook writing only once, as co-author of *The Great Republic*, though successive new editions of that book keep me going back over the material for revisions and updating. In writing that book the difficulty the authors faced was typical: to make it analytic and explanatory—which is to say, intellectually interesting—and yet, at the same time, descriptive in an elementary way. On the whole, I think we succeeded in presenting not only basic information, but a good deal of analysis. But while successful at a certain level, ours is not the kind of book that sweeps the introductory history market. It has done well, and its popularity is increasing. Nevertheless, the deviation from the standard descriptive pattern limited its initial sale.

And what about "recommended reading"?

❦ B. B. ❧ My feeling about this is that the most successful recommendations you can make are those in which you convey your own enthusiasms. If you just list out fifteen books, that doesn't do much for the student. But a few recommendations that convey some of your own particular interests and special enthusiasms can carry the students into the subject, and they can, then, take off on their own. It seems to me that it is necessary to communicate somehow one's own involvement intellectually—or even emotionally at times—to make recommendations effective.

This has dangers, because one's personal responses come out of one's own world, and they therefore don't always carry over to others. There is a book about Irish history that I have recommended to any number of students, a memoir by David Thomson called *Woodbrook*—which is the name of an estate in Ireland where he, as an Oxford history student, came to tutor a young girl and fell in love with both the girl and Ireland. It is a memoir of a love affair, but at the same time, because Thomson is a historian, it is a commentary on Irish history. I think it is a remarkable book, a romantic tale and historically imaginative and interesting. So, when I talk about the way in which seventeenth- and eighteenth-century Irish history telescopes into contemporary Irish problems, I tell students to read Thomson's *Woodbrook*. Some have gone to the book, but a number of them have been rather disappointed—for reasons I don't quite understand. They simply didn't catch my enthusiasm for it.

In graduate school one learns about approaches to and techniques of historical research, interpretation, and writing. But the new Ph.D. will, in all likelihood, have to teach undergraduate students—often in elementary courses. How does he or she prepare for that?

◎ B.B. ◎ Mainly by doing it—by learning from experience. In American universities almost all graduate students are required (often by financial necessity) to teach, mostly in sections of large courses or in undergraduate tutorials. And if they aren't required to do so, they should be.

The natural teachers—those who know their subject thoroughly, care about it, have interesting ideas about it, and have sensitive feedback to other people's responses, verbalized or not—gain confidence quickly after their first classroom encounters, and their skill in teaching nourishes itself. You can't predict—or at least I have never been able to predict accurately—who has the innate ability to reach out to other people, to engage them in the subject, and to help them develop their understanding of it. Again and again I have been amazed at how seemingly shy, apparently unsure people quickly take charge in a classroom, blossom there as nowhere else, and make effective contact with other minds. But some people don't have this ability to start with, and in any case the first classroom encounters can be extremely stressful for anyone.

I remember meeting a close friend of mine, a fellow graduate student—one of the most affable and confidently knowledgeable people I knew, and, at least informally, a natural teacher—after his first class. I asked him how it went. He said it was wonderful. He felt that he had been relaxed, cheerful, and full of ideas, and he was certain that, without much strain, he had got it all across. But he was puzzled, he added, to realize, as he had left the room, that somehow during the hour he had smashed his watch to pieces—and hadn't noticed it. Obviously, it had in fact been a frenzied performance, which must have left his students limp. However, he recovered and soon learned to take it easy. He became a great teacher—a teacher of teachers—and, ultimately, a very successful college president.

But some people don't easily overcome the initial problems, psychological as well as intellectual, of facing a classroom; they don't instinctively know how to gauge other people's responses and how to carry students into the intricacies of a subject without losing their attention. Some of them can be helped. Certain aspects of teaching, I believe—at least in history—can be taught. One can learn from successful models. (I've been fascinated to hear in young historians some of the same intonations and mannerisms, some of the same turns of thought and formulations, that I once heard in their teachers.) Others can help one identify problems and suggest ways of handling them. All sorts of suggestions can be useful— including ones that may seem trivial—in lecturing, as well as in conducting group discussions.

This presumes, of course, some supervision of apprentice teaching, and I think that is where we often fail. We assume anyone can teach, we drop graduate students suddenly into the classroom, largely unsupervised, and we hope for the best. I don't mean that courses in pedagogy should be required. I mean that teachers should be helped by informal counselling, by hints and suggestions that may be useful, and by encouragement to emphasize the most effective parts of their teaching as they develop the style that suits them best.

Nothing can be done without having real control of one's subject, but beyond that lies the mysterious process of conveying one's interest to others, awakening other minds, and leading them into a real engagement with the subject. Some people, I suppose, will never develop that skill, but most people, given intelligent help as they go along, will. And when they do, their satisfaction will equal that of their students. It's such a strange business. Nothing can match the elation of knowing one has succeeded, but neither is there a match for the misery one feels hearing oneself talk and knowing that no one is listening.

With regard to the preparation of America's Ph.D. students in the field of history, what particular importance do you attach to the general examination?

⊙ B.B. ⊙ It is very important, if it is really general. The curse of graduate education in this country is that it is too narrow, too specialized, too parochial—especially in American history. The worst programs are those in American Studies or in the History of American Civilization, in which students are required to take examinations in three or four fields solely in American history, distinguished in various rather arbitrary ways—fields like American social history; literary, intellectual, diplomatic, or religious history; and, for special breadth, something like the history of American architecture or medicine —as if these subjects have nothing much to do with each other or with anything happening elsewhere in the world.

I cannot imagine how anyone can expect to understand American history without seriously studying some other history too—British, continental European, ancient, medieval, far eastern. Partly it's a matter of being able to see significant characteristics by contrast; partly it's a matter of extending one's general historical knowledge; and partly it's a way of seeing something of other historiographical traditions, other approaches to history, other emphases, techniques, forms of documentation, and styles of analysis and writing.

The general exam, if it is properly designed, is the best way to overcome this overspecialization and parochialism. The subject fields involved should be disparate—spread out in time and space—given equal weight and made to cover significant historical periods. One will never again have such an uninterrupted period of concentrated study as one has in preparing for the general exam, and that preparation can be enormously creative, for teaching as well as for later scholarship.

To be able to answer general questions about all of the reading one does, to be able to put together one's own account of large segments of history, from the mass of information available, is excellent basic preparation for teaching. At the most sensitive time in one's professional training, one learns to comprehend—to grasp in their entirety—basic fields of history, not as a mass of technical bibliographies, but as coherent accounts of major passages of human experience. Nothing could be more important.

How do you balance the teaching and the writing of history, as dual elements in what you yourself do?

⊙ B.B. ☉ They are, of course, different elements, but they reinforce each other. Everything I have written I have, first, introduced in the form of teaching. Teaching from my own research is to me fresh, experimental, and intense, and it's particularly valuable to me for two reasons.

First, when you say something aloud—when you say it to another person or, even more, to a group of people— you can hear falsenesses that you otherwise aren't aware of. As a result, you become self-critical in a way that you wouldn't be otherwise. And, second, I have been fortunate in having students, at both undergraduate and graduate levels, who are critical and not shy and who, while on the whole polite, have made clear to me whenever they think I'm on thin ice—when what I'm saying isn't convincing. You get feedback all the time, especially from graduate students, but from undergraduates too. And sometimes (and this can be painful) in reading examination answers, you find what you said simplified to the point of caricature, and you realize how foolish something can sound that you perhaps felt rather proud of.

So, it has been important for me to be able to teach at the same time as I write. The negative side of this is that there are constraints on time and energy. One can't do everything at once; and teaching, I have found—especially undergraduate teaching—is very time-consuming. Doing all this together—teaching, research, and writing—demands time and energy, both of which are limited. But, as I say, that combination, for me at least, has been very useful.

Have there, with the passage of time, been developments that you regard as constituting particular problems within the realm of historical scholarship?

⊚ B.B. ⊚ In the time I have been involved, since just after World War II, it seems to me that one of the most important things that has happened is the vast proliferation of detailed technical studies—very professional, technical monographic writings. And much of this scholarship, valuable in itself, tends to be cast as criticism of some segment of the received tradition, if only because challenges to accepted formulations provide easily constructed formulations and because they are likely to be noticed. As a result, many of the main guidelines or frameworks of large-scale historical interpretation—in American history, in British history, in continental European history—have been undermined and not replaced by anything new.

The great profusion of detailed, critical writing has created gaps in the structure of historical interpretation and shown inconsistencies and weaknesses in what we thought we understood. The longer lines of interpretation have become confused, and the large-scale reconstructions have not been made. It is difficult now for anybody in any major field to keep up with the technical writings, let alone work them back into a clear and consistent narrative. Yet, in the end, that is what has to happen. The details have to be drawn back into some kind of large-scale narrative structure, within which further studies can somehow be integrated.

This is surely one of the most important developments in the recent past. It has happened, for example, in studies of American Puritanism. The professional, scholarly writing on this subject is endless. It has reached the point of scholasticism far beyond anything the Puritans themselves could have coped with. Anybody who writes on Puritanism now has to be expert at a level which, when I was a student of this subject, no one could approach.

The difficulty is how to use, profitably, all the information currently available. What story can now be told that could not have been written earlier? What does it all add up to?

But are all of those "detailed" and "technical" findings really relevant to the large historical picture?

☺ B.B. ☻ Some are not, but some certainly are, and one needs to examine the mass of publications to decide which make a real difference. Certain small-scale, technical micro-studies have transformed large fields. The most famous case I know of is the discovery by Peter Laslett and John Harrison, in Cambridge, England, of the censuses of two tiny inland villages in seventeenth-century England: Clayworth in Nottinghamshire and Cogenhoe in Bedfordshire. From the analysis of the demographic details of these obscure communities came conclusions that, when generalized, transformed much of early modern British social history.

Laslett and Harrison discovered that at least half—probably more than half—of the population of these villages was not still there ten years later. This implied a kind of mobility nobody had dreamed of. (Most historians had previously thought in terms of stable, static, traditional societies.) And they found, also, that while most people lived in large households (six or more persons), the families proper were small (only slightly more than two children each) and consisted of the nuclear group:

husband, wife, and children, together with live-in servants. The traditional idea of the pre-modern family as large, multi-generational, and extended to include more than one married couple wasn't true. Despite the fact that, because of the spread of servitude (ten percent, perhaps more, of the population was in service at some point in their lives), some households were large, families were not.

That study of two very small villages opened up a whole field of local studies, which, in Laslett's research group at Cambridge University, developed into an industry in which an on-going research team studied, and continues to study, every village census they can find. The French were doing this kind of thing before the English, using sophisticated techniques of analysis, which they invented; and they too have transformed the subject on the basis of small-village and regional studies.

The overall story of the development of society at this grass-roots level is still being reconstructed, and many questions remain. The family in the early modern period looks surprisingly modern—surprisingly "nuclear." But what are the boundaries and the turning points of the story of family development as a whole?

Do you think it is today possible to create truly comprehensive historical accounts? Or is there now too much information available for the historian to be able, really, to do this?

❦ B.B. ❧ I have wondered about that, and I some-times conclude that it isn't possible. Yet, I like to think that it is. What we're talking about is reconstructing large-scale narratives of important segments of the his-tory that interests us.

What I am working on at the moment is the devel-opment of the early American population—its recruit-ment and its socio-ethnic characteristics. In this area it is extremely difficult to compose a clear and comprehen-sive narrative. Every time you fit together some small segment of the large story, you find five complications that you hadn't taken account of. And there is a moun-tain of scattered writings, ranging from institutional histories to family genealogies, that have to be consid-ered. The more you know, it seems, the less likely it is that you can put together a convincing picture.

Still, I do think it is possible to reconstruct large nar-ratives. But if you asked why I think so, with all this complexity, I guess I would have to say that it is an arti-cle of faith.

To what extent has the proliferation of technical studies been the result of the emergence of "new technology" within the world of scholarship?

❦ B.B. ❧ New technology, especially computer-based quantitative techniques, has had an important effect. Just as Laslett and the group around him in Cambridge transformed early modern social history in Britain, so the group working on the American South of the seventeenth century, in the Chesapeake area, transformed that subject by technical means that were not available before. They quantified probate records, genealogies, tax records, and church records; and they discovered the means of establishing death rates, birth rates, family structure, and other vital statistics, in such a way that we get a picture of the seventeenth-century South that is far different from anything we had before. It's a grim picture, of desolation, of a death rate far beyond the birth rate: for almost a century the Anglo-American population in the South was not reproducing itself (in fact, it survived only by continuous immigration—waves of new arrivals who repeated the suffering and devastation of their predecessors).

That story, as it emerged from these technical studies of the 1970s and '80s, was absolutely new, and it was made possible by computer analysis. At certain points, of course, the findings become repetitive; new information merely adds elegant refinements. Then, the research becomes mechanical and no longer imaginative—which I think is beginning to happen now. However, there is no question but that this whole area of innovation in historical understanding was made possible by new technology.

Is it the case that much may be lost or overlooked in a

ⓒ B.B. ⓢ I don't see why quantification must ignore time and context, but I do think that there is a distinction between the kind of history that emerges uniquely from quantification and history that derives from more traditional evidence. The former involves, essentially, what I think of as "latent" history; that is, historical events or developments that the participants were not themselves aware of—like shifts in the birth rate (that is obviously very important—everything can turn on that—though the individuals involved at the time are not aware of it; they may be aware of some manifestation or illustration of it within their personal lives, but that's a different story). Most history, however, concerns manifest events, public or private—events that people are keenly aware of, think about, struggle with.

One of the subtler problems now emerging is how to integrate those two levels of historical knowledge into a single whole. It is a difficult technical problem, which is becoming more and more important I think.

How is all this going to affect the writing of history, in a literary way?

ⓒ B.B. ⓢ I wrote a book a few years ago called *Voyagers to the West*. The first one hundred and fifty pages of it are based on numerical tables derived from computer runs. As I began writing that section, I asked myself how this information might lend itself to literary presentation. I decided at the start to try to carry throughout that entire part of the book—all those tables and numbers—a single literary image, an image of the progressive clarification of an immensely detailed panoramic painting, like the exquisitely detailed backgrounds of fifteenth-century Flemish pictures—as if the numbers in table after table revealed in patches, one after another, the segments of this intricate background. I felt that, in the end, the whole panorama would be revealed.

In the first draft I had all this rather elaborately worked out, but ultimately I had to cut down the imagery, because it seemed too self-conscious and insistent; the reader would become more concerned with the author than the subject. But that image is still there, in modified form.

In general, you try, by any means you can devise, to use numbers as descriptive data and to tie them into the narrative account, as you would any other kinds of data.

In quantitative history one commonly finds phrases like "as Table 14 indicates" or "analysis of this table reveals"—which is scarcely literary. Does not quantification necessarily alter verbal usages?

❦ B.B. ❧ That kind of historical writing ceases to be a

literary expression and becomes a kind of social-science research report. Thus, as you say: "Column 4, Table 7, shows the following . . . " (present tense for the verb "show"), in much the way a sociologist would report on statistical information about group interaction or an experimental psychologist would report on cognition speeds. That is the language of the behavioral sciences, in which one "writes up" the results of experiments, based on pre-formulated hypotheses; one checks the experimental data to see if they confirm the theory. But that is not historical writing, at least I hope it isn't.

With so much statistical data now available, is there a problem of the historian's becoming absorbed not in human problems of the past, but in the methodological problems of the modern historian?

⟨ B.B. ⟩ Yes, that danger exists, but one can avoid it, and use numbers to deepen one's understanding of human problems. For example, in the sources I used in writing *Voyagers to the West* (which is a study of about ten thousand people who went from Britain to America in the years 1773–1776), I had a lot of information about each person: age, sex, occupation, where he or she came from, family groups, reasons for leaving. All that information was assembled and entered on computer tapes.

You look at the computer runs, and you say, "Well, there are so-and-so many people of such an age, place, occupation, and purpose." Then, you start to go deeper, probing the backgrounds and destinies of the people the statistics have identified, and you work out a general picture of the lives of these people, keeping an eye out for important similarities and differences. Categories form; you begin to see patterns.

It turned out that there was not one, but two movements of people, mingled together in the data. The family configurations, ages, occupations, et cetera, fitted two separate pictures; and that difference formed the structure of a story that could, then, be examined exhaustively, by deeper research, at the individual, "micro" level. Once the overall pattern was clear, I went into the backgrounds of these two quite different groups of people—into the contexts of individual lives—to explain and illustrate the different patterns.

The numbers become signals to lead one far more deeply into human realities than one could otherwise have gone. If it is just enumeration, it's not history; it's numbers. In the end, one must talk about people, their activities and concerns.

Can you give an example of this new approach to social history, which tends to deal with people in general and with long-term trends? Are there peculiar difficulties in this kind of history?

    ❦ B.B. ❦ One of the most famous, most intricate and

well-developed, examples is that concerning the profitability of slavery. That has been tested by Robert Fogel and others—very expert quantifiers and great computer experts and statisticians. Fogel and his collaborators have published volume after volume on this problem, using every available record in the South, trying to discover whether slavery was profitable, whether it destroyed the black family, and whether slaves' material lives were worse than those of free industrial workers—questions of the greatest importance, which bear heavily on morality and on the origins of the Civil War. Their answers, in large measure, are that, yes, under certain circumstances slavery was profitable, that it did not destroy the slaves' family life, and in material (not psychological) terms slaves were not worse off than free laborers. But the difficulty with such interpretation of overall profitability is that the planters themselves couldn't have known it. They didn't have computers or any long-term statistical measurements. They had to make their own rough calculations for their own plantations and decide as best they could what to do. And the slaves couldn't have known how wretched the free laborers were, nor would they, who lived under the constant threat of physical brutality, have cared much if they had known.

What Fogel was doing was getting the long-term, latent development laid out in quantitative terms—laid out in a context of information and comprehension that the participants themselves did not have—and then he and his collaborators tried to integrate the quantitative data with the manifest politics, morality, and family life of the time.

To what extent do you think the proliferation of that kind of social history is driven by political ideology derived from present-day moral concerns centering on the "underclass" in modern life?

❦ B.B. ❦ Current political and social concerns have raised important questions about the historical development of ordinary working people—about mass phenomena. These questions are not new, though they may be more intense now than before; but they have generated a great deal of new writing, in part because of newly available techniques of historical study. Without quantitative analysis—with only literary impressionism—there is no way of getting at the real history of the mass base of the population; you couldn't really demonstrate what had happened. This newly available information can have important political implications. One can now usefully ask what the fate of ordinary people has been—whether conditions have improved or worsened—and this can be highly "relevant" to current politics and to concern with the problems of the underclass.

Yes, political and ideological concerns have undoubtedly stimulated historical research and writing. They always have. But there are problems involved. Most historical issues are generated from within historical study itself. Perceptive historians, immersed in their materials, note gaps in our knowledge that should be filled and anomalies in the data—inconsistencies and discrepancies—which impel them or others to find explanations. In the documentation and in the existing literature they see connections, parallels, and implications that suggest new patterns, whole worlds, large or small, that have not been seen before. They have an intellectual—but not a political or ideological—stake in the outcome. They don't insist that the explanations come out in a particular way, only that the discrepancies be reconciled, the open questions answered, and the newly perceived worlds explored and explained. Historians motivated chiefly by political and ideological concerns, however, commonly *do* have a stake in the outcome. They are not simply satisfying their curiosity or the desire to reveal lost worlds. They want the story to prove something, to support certain policies, to send certain messages. They are likely, therefore, if only unconsciously, to exaggerate or otherwise bias the stories they tell.

There are many historians now who are concerned to show the innateness, depth, and historical rootedness of modern American problems: public problems with moral dimensions—poverty, social (including gender) inequalities, racism. For them, it is important to be able to show that there is something immemorial, intrinsic in American life—a deep strain—that has always led to these kinds of problems or that there was once a better world from which at some point we departed. They keep reading present attitudes toward these issues back into the past, as if they were *then* contemporary. But past generations may not have experienced things that way, may well have focussed on different issues—not necessarily better issues, but different ones.

Still, political commitments generate enormous power in historical study—as I say, they always have. One hopes that in the end the sheer competition among historians, their increasing sophistication, and the growing density of documentation will keep the political biases in some kind of control.

Are not historians supposed to be concerned with things that are urgent issues in their own time, seen historically? Yes, of course, but in a way that does not violate the texture of the past, that does not telescope past and present. The task is to look at these issues in their own context.

Is this a generational problem? Looking at ourselves historically, can one say there has developed a new professional ethic that places less emphasis on context and more emphasis on moral judgement?

☙ B.B. ❧ I think we have a deeper contextual sense than historians in the past have had. But at the same time, in certain areas, I think there is a heightening of moral concerns in history. I think both are going on currently. One can, therefore, optimistically say that it may all be to the good, because you then get a richer compound in historical study than you had before. I agree, so long as one preserves, above all, knowledge of what that past time and those past events were really like.

You have been talking just now about new kinds of documentation—numbers, statistics, and the like. But historical evidence exists, of course, in many different forms. Are there observations you would make about the historian's use of other forms or kinds of sources?

☸ B.B. ☸ The history of historical writings shows a succession of different forms of evidence, interpretation, argument, and proof. Various eras have developed different forms of evidence, and all of them must be used critically. For example, to go far back into medieval history, the saints' lives—which are an important genre of documentation—turn out to be, for us, two-level phenomena. On the one hand, they contain objective biographical facts about the saints, witnessed by the writers or conveyed to them more or less accurately by legend. But, on the other hand, in order to establish their subjects' sainthood, the writers select events (miracles, prophecies, et cetera) that fit the assumed characteristics of what saints are expected to do or be—hence convey the notions of sainthood accepted in the writers' time.

And they also reflect, however dimly, the distinctive interests and personalities of the writers, as well as something of their general mental world. In these texts, fact and fiction are interwoven in a two-dimensional pattern. Somehow the modern medievalist must sort all this out: establish the objective biographical information and identify the formulas of sainthood recognized in the writers' time and some of the characteristics of the mental world of the monkish intelligentsia responsible for writing these tales. Experts have spent much time and effort on working all this out. Some of the methodological writings on the saints' lives—especially that of an Israeli scholar, Aviad Kleinberg—are remarkably subtle.

There is also a vivid and amusing exaggeration of these hagiographical tales in Thomas Mann's wonderful novel (half novel, half spoof of the medieval saints' lives) *The Holy Sinner.* It's a grotesque, tongue-in-cheek Oedipal account of the semi-mythical Pope, Saint Gregory, based on the fantasies of the twelfth-century poet Hartmann von Aue. It's about Gregory's supposedly incestuous origins and equally incestuous marriage; his fourteen-year penance on a rock in the ocean, nourished by mysterious earth fluids, during which time he turned into a hedgehog; his ultimate redemption and his restoration to human form; his reception of grace; his becoming pope and saint; and the absolution he gave to his mother, with whom he had lived in sin.

Mann, typically, in order to create irony and distance,

and to give the medieval legend verisimilitude, put the telling of the story in the mouth of a later, credulous, naive, and rather appealing humanist monk, who partly believes and partly disbelieves the mythological details of Gregory's early life. Mann takes the curse off the fantasies—makes them more believable—by putting the story into the mouth of this simple humanist, and by doing so he establishes three levels.

There is a credulous story-telling monk—an Irishman, quite properly, since more saints' lives were written in medieval Ireland than elsewhere in Europe—who reveals himself and the culture of his time as he talks on, naively, about the ancient saint. Then, there is the saint himself, who did have obscure, somewhat mysterious origins and did become Pope. And behind it all is Mann, immensely sophisticated, having fun with the whole business of stories within stories, and incidentally playing all sorts of games with medieval languages and the symbolism of names, many of them taken from the original Parsifal legend and Gregorovius's history of the city of Rome. Scholars have worked themselves into a lather trying to uncover Mann's sources and explain the games he played with them. It's an extravagant, at times hilarious example of what medievalists dealing with the saints' lives have to contend with: trying to uncover several layers of reality through the accounts of monkish story-tellers whose commitment to historical "truth," as we know it, did not exist.

Sources are always changing and are always suspect. Newspapers became a source of evidence in the eighteenth century, but they too have to be used critically and cautiously. Eighteenth-century newspapers were very often hack work by hired writers. If you think of the eighteenth-century newpapers as small versions of today's *New York Times*, you're in trouble—because they weren't. Most of them, financed by partisan interests, didn't even pretend to objectivity. Their printers had their own agendas, and the modern historian must use them partly for the information they contain about the events that they describe and partly, too, as evidence of their writers' biases and agendas.

Photographs are an immensely valuable historical resource. They were used brilliantly in the recent Civil War series shown on public television. But the difficulty with photographs, which are obviously vivid, is that they have no dynamics. They are static moments. You don't know how that moment was formed, and you don't see the way in which it would subsequently shift and what would develop from it. Much of the visual power of that Civil War television series came from the producers' ability to use their camera dynamically. They let it cross a panoramic scene slowly—or go back and forth—so as to give it a dynamic quality it didn't really have.

As for oral history, which ethnographic historians are using more and more now, taking over techniques from the anthropologists, that has its own problems. I am by no means an expert in this field, but one of the problems certainly is the fact that to reconstruct past circumstances from oral traditions that have lasted into the present —passed orally from generation to generation (as opposed to oral history in the sense of one individual's testimony regarding occurrences that he or she personally experienced)—you somehow have to take account of the flow of history between those events and the present speakers in that tradition. For example, the strange circumstances of Captain Cook's death in 1779 in Hawaii have become the subject of intense examination and subtle interpretation by distinguished anthropologists— Marshall Sahlins in Chicago and Greg Dening in Australia. Their interpretations are based in large part on reconstructions of eighteenth-century Polynesian religious practices, deduced from what Polynesians in our own time retain in their culture as oral traditions. How accurately that reflects patterns of behavior as they were two hundred years ago and how far ethnographic history is an unverifiable projection of ethnographers' ways of thinking are real questions, which seem to me to be difficult to answer.

My point is that new forms of evidence are discovered or devised, but they have to be used quite critically. While one is enthusiastic at the beginning about how much one can do with a new form of documentation, in the end one has to be aware of the limitations and problems that are involved in using it.

Then, establishing the validity of recorded data is one of the great challenges for the historian?

❦ B.B. ❧ That is one of the most important parts of the craft; namely, to be critical of sources. It is something that the medievalists and those who work on diplomatic exchanges have been most keenly aware of—the need for critical analysis of documentary evidence. The difficulty comes up in a different form in modern social history, where you're dealing with masses of data. Computer data can be very hard to interpret, even if one is sure of the statistical methods required.

I had an amusing experience in this connection. My wife and I did a book based on computer print-outs, back when computer facilities were extremely primitive. This was in the mid-'50s. (The computer we used, by the way, if it still exists, would be considered proper for the Smithsonian museum. In fact, the book we wrote is occasionally cited in the histories of quantification, to show how naive the beginnings of the process were.) Nevertheless, we did this study, *Massachusetts Shipping, 1697–1714*, which was innovative at the time, composing tables from a tabulator. The machine ran punched cards over sensors consisting of wire brushes, so that the brushes made contact through the holes, and those contact points printed out numbers. From those runs we made up the tables for the book.

One of the tables that came out was so fascinating—so

unexpected—that we couldn't believe how original we were. But when we looked at it more closely and compared it with other tables and with some of the background material available, it became clear that it was not so much fascinating as fantastic. It was crazy. We tried to reconstruct what had happened, and we discovered (with some expert help) that a wire in one of the brushes had become bent away from the rest of the wires that made up that brush, and so it registered the holes in the wrong column. Our miraculous table was based on the wrong numbers. We explained all this in a footnote in the book, suggesting the dangers of the work we were so heroically engaged in.

My point, again, is that new materials and new historical evidence come up repeatedly, and they have to be used critically as sources, because each has dangers that need to be carefully assessed.

A few moments ago, in referring to the pursuit of historical scholarship, you used the word "craft." How do you relate considerations of craft to history?

☺ B.B. ☺ History, as written and taught, *is* a craft, though it can be much more. At its best it can be an art form. It has scientific aspects, too, with respect to certain more or less agreed-on criteria of proof and to the use of certain mechanical techniques. But, it seems to me it must at least be a craft, in the sense that the skills involved can be learned—that the practices involved are tested through time and that practitioners know, more or less, whether a certain presentation, analysis, proof, or documentary interpretation is sound or not.

Like any other craft, standards of quality can be recognized among those who practice it. That is why it seems to me the guildlike training in the graduate schools, when it is handled right, makes sense. That's how craft skills have been developed and tested through the ages. Therefore, it seems to me that while, as I say, history can be much more, the main body of historical writing and teaching will be a craft product.

Although the areas or subject matter of history are infinitely varied and diverse, are there guiding principles and means or methods of approach that are generally common to all historical concerns?

⊙ B. B. ⊙ Common problems? Universal concerns of the craft? There seems to me to be one that runs through the whole historical enterprise: the problem of anachronism.

All historians are involved in this question; namely, whether or not one's present views are read back into the past and, therefore, whether the past is distorted, foreshortened, and its distinctiveness lost. That seems to me a universal and basic problem of historical writing and teaching.

Without presenting the past in the correct context of

its own time, and somehow disengaging it from one's present—without grasping the past as the present it once was—one can never understand what really happened or how that distant present changed into a later present and, eventually, into the present that we ourselves are experiencing.

The past is not only distant, it is in various ways a different world. The basic experiences are different from ours, yet they seemed to the people who experienced them then to be so normal that they did not record things that we would consider to be strange and particularly interesting. For example, sanitation. I've wondered how people in the eighteenth century dealt with human waste. How was it handled in the cities?

I know of very few studies of this question, for any period. Alex Scobie wrote an excellent piece on it in the Roman world, and what he found was appalling; Fernand Braudel discussed it briefly for sixteenth- and seventeenth-century Europe; Donald Reid wrote a book on the Paris sewers in the nineteenth century; and there is a remarkable piece by James Clifford on eighteenth-century London. Clifford, a distinguished literary historian, for years studied the life and works of Samuel Johnson, and in the course of his research apparently kept notes on every reference he found to the sanitation problem in London. The picture he finally described in an article based on those notes is fascinating—and, like Scobie's, rather horrifying.

Similarly, did clothing itch? That can't be trivial. In the Chesapeake region in the seventeenth century, the clothes commonly worn by people who worked in the open fields were made of what was called "linsey-woolsey," a mixture of wool and linen. On hot days that cloth must have felt like a combination of burlap and sandpaper. I can't imagine how they got through the summers. Yet, I don't know of a single reference, in the historical sources, as to whether the clothing itched or burned.

So, too, it is difficult to find a classicist who can tell one, right off, whether the apartments in the big buildings in ancient Rome had doors. This seems to me important. If you can't close the door, it's a very different world from one in which that is possible.

Huizinga mentions in the beginning of his famous book, *The Waning of the Middle Ages*, that if one walked into a medieval town one would be struck by the noise, the constant sound of bells. But what would strike me most, I think, would be the smell. Those towns and villages must have stunk.

What I am suggesting is that these are the vital commonplaces of everyday life, though nobody wrote much about them, and it is very hard to extract information about them from the records that survive. I'm sure there are things in our life too that later historians will wonder about, but which we are not recording.

It is even more difficult in intellectual life, where you

have to work your way back into another way of thinking, into the mentality of a lost world. There are historians who have done this. I have already mentioned Peter Brown, who I think has done this, and some French historians—Guy Thuillier, for example—have gone deep into personal and local histories to find the feel and color and sound of life in the past. But this is extremely difficult to do.

So, the first thing about trying to avoid anachronism is to recognize that the past is not only distant, but different, and that it takes a great effort of imagination and substantial knowledge to get back into such remote experiences.

A second problem in trying to avoid anachronism, I've already touched on; that is, the great difficulty, in tracing public events (politics, wars, depressions, and other concerns that fill the headlines), of overcoming the knowledge of the outcome. This is one of the great impediments to a truly contextual history. Somehow one has to recapture, and build into the story, contemporaries' ignorance of the future. I wish I were sure how to do this properly. But one tries. One stresses the contingencies—looks for the accidents of the time and tries to avoid assigning the heroism or villainy that was unclear at the time but that was determined by the later outcomes. And, if possible, one gives a sympathetic account of the losers. If one can, up to a certain point, work sympathetically with the losers, one can—in some small part at least—overcome the knowledge of the outcome.

In your book The Ideological Origins of the American Revolution *you describe in terms of a set of mental perceptions the dynamics of the urge to separate from Britain. But have not some historians felt that this centers the whole consideration on an elitist world, a world of thinkers, as opposed to the relatively deprived masses?*

☉ B.B. ☉ Yes, but the differences between mass and elite perceptions tend to disappear when one really enters into the interior lives of the people involved, and when one concentrates, as I have tried to do, not on the history of ideas as such—not on formal intellectual discourse—but on states of mind, mental maps of the world: the patterns of ideas, beliefs, fears, and aspirations that define our perceptions of the world and shape our responses to events. There is nothing elitist about that. I was trying to describe not the systematic, logical mental structures of philosophers, but the mind-set of the people who led the Revolution—merchants, politicians, planters, and preachers. Their general views and attitudes were very broadly shared.

The real difficulty is not how to relate the views of political leaders to those of the general political population, but how to reach back to that distant era and recapture the states of mind that then existed. That kind of historical penetration is extremely difficult to manage. It is part of the basic problem of recovering past contexts.

As I said before, one never can, completely, overcome this problem. And one of the most important reasons for this inescapable limitation is that you, as historian, as opposed to the distant participants, know how it all came out. The people of the time did *not* know how it would come out, and that uncertainty is a profound element in the past, which the poor historian can only grope to understand. And the more distant you are, the more difficult the problem.

It takes great skill, knowledge, and imagination to re-capture mentalities of the deeper past—those of classical antiquity, for example. Some historians have succeeded. Peter Brown's biography of St. Augustine is a brilliant book about a vastly different world from ours, a world I can just barely grasp. But, if you ask me how I know Brown's book is good, how I know that what he says corresponds to a very distant reality, I can only say that he has got the documentation, that the objective details he presents add up consistently to the general picture he conveys, that as far as I can tell what he says matches what else is known, and that as I read the book I simply feel that he describes a real world, that he recaptures some of the physical reality of the early-Christian and the late-Roman world and essential elements of the state of mind of people at that time and place. There are others who manage to do this, but not many.

Is not that "recapturing of reality" what your The Ordeal of Thomas Hutchinson *undertakes to do, a book about a leader of the colonial opposition to the American Revolution?*

✪ B.B. ✪ Because the materials were there, in Hutchinson's many personal letters and in public documents, I thought I could get back into his state of mind; that is, into the mind of the most important loser in the Revolution. (Who else really lost? Britain flourished after the Revolution, and so, too, did America. The only complete losers were the American Tories, who were despised even in Britain.) And studying the losers sympathetically is a way of overcoming our present knowledge of the outcome. Hutchinson might well have had a different reputation and a different role in history if Britain had won the war.

What would have happened if America had lost the Revolution—which was the outcome most people expected? One can only guess. Perhaps George Washington would have become a figure like Robert E. Lee—a wonderful man who quietly disappeared after the Civil War, serving loyally as president of Washington College in Lexington, Virginia, shunning publicity and obedient to civil authority, hoping in this way to help restore the fortunes of the South.

There is no better example of the vital element of uncertainty in the past—which, as I have emphasized, historians can never fully recapture—than what is happening at this very moment: this evening, January 16, 1991. As we all know, one hour ago (the morning of January seventeenth in the Middle East) American planes began bombing Iraq. But as we speak here tonight, no one on earth knows what the outcome will be. Just before we began this conversation, someone asked me what a historian in the year 2050 will say about the origins of the war with Iraq. I said that that is an impossible question to answer, because the historian of 2050 will know, as we do not know, how it all came out and what the long-term consequences proved to be. The eventual interpretation will be based on that outcome.

The deepest context of our present situation, which later historians will hope to understand, is precisely the uncertainty we feel tonight. Will the air war succeed? Will a ground war be necessary? Will Saddam Hussein's army live up to its reputation and exact a terrible toll in American lives? Or will they fail, and will Americans and their allies simply sweep through to Baghdad? Or will something completely different happen, something we cannot now imagine? Future historians certainly will know the answers before they write a word about this war, and they will read that knowledge back to give an account of how the result emerged through clear stages of development, reducing the alternative outcomes to triviality.

The great uncertainty of what we are all experiencing

this evening, at this moment, is an almost unrecoverable reality.

With respect to the difficulty of recovering historical contexts, to the extent that one succeeds in doing this, are there further problems that follow?

☉ B.B. ☉ To the extent that you succeed, you run into two kinds of problems. First, you can find yourself facing what is essentially a moral problem, because to explain—in depth and with sympathy—is, implicitly at least, to excuse. One could, for example, spend quite some time explaining the very sensible—logical—reasons why Jefferson did not free his slaves and why the Constitution did not eliminate slavery. But it seems to be moral obtuseness to say that Jefferson and the framers of the Constitution had their reasons for this. However sensible those reasons may have been, to try to explain them seems to be an attempt to excuse them, while what historians, according to some, should be doing is condemning them and focussing on the obvious immorality of slavery.

Jefferson was a very right-minded, liberal, civil, imaginative, and sensitive man, and he sincerely loathed slavery; he called it "an abominable crime" and a blot on civilization. Why didn't he free his slaves? Why didn't Madison? Consistent with the Revolution's egalitarianism, there was an abolitionist movement during those years; surely it should have been advanced and exploited by people like Jefferson. Yet, what strikes one forcibly is not that Jefferson's generation did not get rid of slavery, but that so much was done at that time to eliminate it, even if it wasn't completely outlawed.

Slavery *was* prohibited in five states of the Old Northwest, and the northeastern states either eliminated it or set in motion laws that would in time eliminate it. Above all, a problem was created out of this that never existed before the Revolution. Before the Revolution, slavery was rarely seen as a problem. After the Revolution, there never was a time when it wasn't a problem. And that seems to me a tremendous transformation of the whole issue. However, some would say that since they came so close to eliminating slavery, it is morally obtuse to explain that there are reasons for it to have survived. It doesn't seem good enough to say that the people who wrote the Constitution were more concerned about creating and sustaining the fragile Union than of running the risk of destroying it over the issue of slavery; to suggest they knew what they were talking about is, somehow, to exonerate the evil of slavery.

To put all of this in basic terms: In a deep contextualism you run into a moral problem, because you are not merely explaining; you are also, as I said a few moments ago, to some degree—if only implicitly—excusing what people did in the past. If you think that part of the job of a historian is to judge what people have done, you've made it very difficult to do that, if you stick to a strict contextualism.

You said there were two problems in recovering past contexts. What is the second?

⊙ B.B. ◎ The second problem is that, in explaining how things were, how things functioned, one tends to lose the dynamics. The disturbing elements, the disequilibrating forces, the motives for change, are by definition subordinated in any situation you describe, since it is the stable—that is, the dominant—elements you must describe. If you give a fully contextual picture of what was going on at a particular time, by definition the disturbing elements that will lead to change are subordinated to the stable elements. Therefore, how can you show why things changed?

There are vivid illustrations of this. Australia's historians, for example, celebrated their bicentennial in 1988 by publishing a multi-volume history of Australia, and they did this in an unusual way. Australia was colonized by the British in January 1788. So, the historians devoted a volume to Australia as it existed in that year. Then, subsequent volumes were devoted to similar cross-sections, or deep probes, at fifty-year intervals after 1788. These are remarkable volumes that cover all aspects of Australian life in those years—everything that was going on in the politics, culture, economy, society, et cetera in the selected years, and all the connections among these aspects of life. But there is no indication of how or why Australia *changed* between 1788 and 1838 or between 1888 and 1938. What were the dynamics? You understand what Australian life was like in 1838, but it's accidental if you can see why 1888 was so different. The volumes are not organized to explain the dynamics of history. One Australian historian, Graeme Davison, has described the theory behind this work, but I think the problem of explaining change remains. One finds suggestions only in the interstices of what they wrote.

Or come closer to home. If I can give a convincing account of Thomas Hutchinson; if I can show that he was not a fool, not disloyal to his own people, and not morally blind; if I can explain convincingly why he did what he did; how can I explain the movement of events that overwhelmed him, by-passed him, swept him and his world into oblivion? Concentrating on the context of things as they were—on the functional, interlocking mesh of circumstance—how can I explain why anything changed?

At the end of my Hutchinson book I tried to do this by saying that for all his ability and his love for his country, he wasn't sufficiently aware of—didn't respond to —certain elements in his own society that others were becoming committed to, and that those elements which, for temperamental and circumstantial reasons, he didn't grasp—created the future. But the strength of the Hutchinson book, such as it is, lies in a sympathetic picture of his life and views, and the dynamics of the time can only be discussed in the margins. That side of the story—what I have called "the contagion of liberty": the propelling force of liberal aspirations, which in effect created the future—had to be developed in another book.

The English historian A. J. P. Taylor once put the problem dramatically: If one concentrates on the functioning of political and social institutions at given moments in the past, without accounting at the same time for the force of dynamic ideas and movements, one will end up with history that is not merely Tory, but Byzantine.

But do not the dynamic forces also have a context that accounts for their success? You seem to suggest that in your early article in the American Historical Review, *"Enlightenment Thought and Political Experience in Eighteenth-Century America," which is an account of the peculiar force of circumstance that propelled certain ideas and aspirations forward. What you describe there is almost a model of change.*

☙ B. B. ❧ In that essay I tried to explain why the ideas and attitudes that eventually became the basic political ideology of this country, and which were derived from a minority tradition in Britain, caught on so powerfully here in the eighteenth century. I tried to explain that the circumstances were different from Britain's, in ways that made the reception of these ideas strongly positive. In England, the circumstances were negative.

Later, I tried to explain this in greater detail in *The Origins of American Politics*. I hope I succeeded in showing how certain circumstances could have an impelling effect on historical developments that were already in motion, but which were hitherto constrained and limited. But, however you tackle it, there is a persistent problem of introducing motion into a still picture of a distant world, of explaining how and why it changed.

In the history of New England a major issue is the conflicts between the Native Americans and the English settlers. Although it may be possible to bring together the viewpoints of the English settlers into a general English perspective of the time, how can one establish an Indian perspective? And how does one reconcile those two perspectives?

❦ B.B. ❦ That's terribly difficult. Only one set of actors in this situation left behind an articulated record of their thoughts, in their own words. There is very little direct documentation of the Indians' interior point of view. All one can do is follow the anthropologists in extracting scraps of data from the records we do have (the more objective and accidentally recorded the better), piece them together into as cohesive a picture as one can make, and take oral tradition seriously.

Some historians have done this remarkably well: Helen Rountree's book on the Powhatans, for example; Daniel Richter on the Iroquois; James Merrell on the Catawbas; Richard White's *Middle Ground*, about the Huron tribes. And there is a mass of scattered information developed by the anthropologists and gathered into compilations like the Smithsonian's *Handbook of North American Indians*. Even so, we have very limited access to the natives' private, inner world. We are just beginning to learn how to deal with this problem, which in the end may never be fully solved.

As to the reconciliation of the two perspectives, the historian is indeed trying to present the whole picture sympathetically, from both sides. The differences between the two viewpoints can become major historical facts and need to be fully understood. A successful account, like Richard White's book, which I just mentioned, encompasses both sides sympathetically, and it identifies the critical points of congruence and conflict, as well as the shifting relations between the two. Hence the book's title—which perhaps more accurately should be *The Failure of the Middle Ground*.

In some areas of the world that were colonized by Europeans, one can come closer to working out a truly bifocal history—one that incorporates with equal sensitivity the viewpoints and experiences of both native and conquering peoples, and that explains the interaction between them. New Zealand, for example. That country's historians and anthropologists—Anne Salmond, in particular—have been quite successful in explaining both perspectives. The main reason for their success, I think, is the relative size of the surviving native population. The Maoris, in modern New Zealand, are fifteen times more numerous, relative to the population as a whole, than the Indians in the United States. And among the Maoris are distinguished scholars, jurists, and community leaders who have brought their native culture, with its powerful oral traditions, into the mainstream of the nation's intellectual and social life.

But are there systematic, logical problems in presenting a bifocal or multifocal history? At one level, no. The same events or circumstances can be narrated in separate sequences from several points of view, each of them as reliable, objectively verifiable, and contextual as the others. Mack Walker's recent book on the expulsion of the Protestants from the Archbishopric of Salzburg in 1732—an event that resounded throughout western Christendom—is an excellent example. He tells the story from the point of view, first, of the Archbishopric; then, of the Kingdom of Prussia, to which most of the Protestants fled; then, of the Holy Roman Empire, of which Salzburg was a part; and, finally, of the emigrants themselves (whose travels and travails, incidentally, were recorded in an extraordinary series of paintings and engravings wonderfully reproduced in a book by Angelika Marsch). As Walker writes in his preface: to say that there are many different truths in the same series of events, that the story can be told, accurately, from different points of view, is not to say that there is no truth at all or that false stories are as legitimate as true ones. The systematic problem arises if one tries to incorporate all the different points of view, all the different stories, within a single narrative structure—not sandwiching them in, one after the other, in repeated sequences, but telling the tale only once, in a single inclusive narrative.

Have you any observations to make regarding the field of "women's history," which has emerged as an area of specialization during the past two or three decades?

 B.B. One of the great developments in the recent expansion of historical knowledge is the amount we have learned about women in history—not so much as we should know; we're still trying to establish some basic facts. But for the first time we are beginning to know something very substantial about this whole area of history, and that development comes out of all sorts of impulses and desires. One stimulus lies simply in the increasing availability of source material. The huge and growing accumulation of historical documentation on the history of women in Radcliffe's Schlesinger Library, for example, invites and stimulates study. Then, of course, the feminist movement has greatly intensified an interest in the subject.

The result is that we're turning up things all the time about women in history, things that will add materially to the general story. Again, however, as in so many other "new" areas, this adds to the complexity of the general story and to the difficulty of writing comprehensive historical narratives. My sense of this is that, so far, the available material on women's history has not yet been drawn fully into general history. It still remains somewhat parochial, somewhat polemical. It's still coming out, in part, as an argument, rather than as a natural part of the wider story. Some feminists want to keep it that way, develop it that way, on the theory that any general account will inevitably be male-dominated and that a true feminist history, based on a feminist epistemology, will be an ideological weapon for women's full liberation. But less-ideological historians will hope to integrate the history of women into general interpretations of the past.

Occasionally one sees a book referred to (perhaps most commonly in promotional text prepared by its publisher) as being "definitive" with respect to its subject matter. What do you think about "definitiveness" with respect to historical or biographical works?

❦ B.B. ❧ Large subjects in history can never be definitively written. There is no definitive history of the Civil War, and there never will be. Such a vast, complex event lends itself to a series of questions that is endless, and those questions are phrased and rephrased, generation after generation, according to contemporary interests. Certain limited aspects of the Civil War can be written of in a way that might be called "definitive"—its origins, the planning of various campaigns, certain battles and logistical problems—but not the Civil War as a whole.

Similarly, one can more or less definitively explain the origins and character of the thirteenth, fourteenth, and fifteenth amendments to the U.S. Constitution; but "Reconstruction," on the other hand, is a problem of a different order—as is the French Revolution, the origins of Christianity, et cetera. If one wants to establish the circumstances of Franklin D. Roosevelt's death, one can perhaps do this definitively—though even that kind of event may not in all cases be definitively described. It seems there will never be an end to the question of John F. Kennedy's death, just as there will always be people who insist that one of the Czar's family escaped assassination by the Bolsheviks.

The point is, that when you go beyond factual reestablishment into the interpretation of large subjects, there is no definitive history. It is impossible, and should be impossible, because history is a way of answering questions about the past—questions which together explain how we got to be the way we are—and the explanations of the great transitional developments will shift according to our current interests and criteria of proof.

It all depends on the scope of the inquiry and on the information available. In limited areas, with set terms of reference and enough information, yes: as I have said, you can come up with some kind of account that might be regarded as definitive. But large subjects can never be definitively, finally described.

The characterization that someone is a "popular" historian or "popular" biographer is often used in a derogatory, patronizing, or dismissive sense. Have you any observations on this?

☯ B.B. ☯ I hope that every good historian is, in at least some of the things he or she does, "popular." History is not an esoteric subject, the preserve of scholarly mandarins. It is, or should be, public knowledge, and the broader, the more popular the audience for accurate history, the better. People will always have some sense of the past—usually a jumble of facts, myths, and vague images—which shapes their view of themselves and the world around them. The question is whether the popular sense of the past is reasonably accurate, free at least of wishful fantasies, and so more likely to keep people from repeating the mistakes and disasters of the past. The difficulty is that good history has to be based on technical details, has to be balanced and nuanced, while popular history has to be written with verbal flair, with wit, imagination, and a compelling style. The combination of the two—details, nuance, and balance, on the one hand; and literary flair, on the other—is rare. But it can be done.

One can think of examples: Arthur Schlesinger's *Age of Jackson* and Oscar Handlin's *The Uprooted*. Both of them were very popular books; and while both of them have been challenged on technical grounds by later historians, they conveyed revealing accounts of important passages of the past to a very large number of people. Similarly, Emmanuel LeRoy Ladurie's *Montaillou*, a meticulously documented study of the life and culture of an obscure mountain village in southern France in the early-fourteenth century, has been immensely popular, not only in France, but throughout Europe. There is no systematic reason why good history can't be popular, but it seldom is, simply because, as I say, it is so difficult to maintain the historian's discipline and at the same time make the story compelling and broadly accessible.

What are your thoughts regarding "historical fiction"?

 B.B. There is "historical fiction" and there is something one might call "history as fiction." As to the first, historical novelists can greatly extend their readers' interest in history. There isn't the slightest doubt that a novelist like Walter Scott had a tremendous influence on historical awareness generally and that he stimulated some very serious historians, amateur and professional.

John Clive's biography of Macaulay is particularly interesting in this connection. Macaulay, probably the greatest nineteenth-century historian in the English-speaking world, was immersed in historical novels when he was young. In fact, what Clive isolated as the critical point of Macaulay's development was his creation of a kind of fantasy world, based on the historical novels that he and his sisters indulged in as children. Historical fiction stimulated him, as it would stimulate many others. In a sense, all of this early romanticizing of the past lay behind Macaulay's massive *History of England*.

Some historical novels are very good background history; they can convey the general character, the atmosphere of a past era. One of my favorites is Zoë Oldenbourg's *The World Is Not Enough*, a novel about France in the thirteenth century—about the Crusades. It seems to me to be an excellent fictional account of the society and daily life of that time, based on a great deal of study on Oldenbourg's part. And other novelists more distinguished than Oldenbourg have written excellent history, as incidental elements of their fiction. They did this not by fictionalizing famous historical figures, which can be awful—("Marquis, who is that tall red-headed American over there? Thomas something? Johnson? Jefferson? And what is that declaration sticking out of his pocket?" That kind of thing, in books or at the theatre or on television, makes me cringe.)—but by conveying the quality of life in the past.

My two favorite modern novelists, Patrick White and Thomas Mann, both did this wonderfully. (Maybe that's why I like them so much.) There is no better, more accurate and moving account of farm settlement in the Australian outback in the early-twentieth century than White's *The Tree of Man*, nor of the brutality of the encounter between Victorian Britons and the aborigines than his *A Fringe of Leaves*. Similarly accurate is Mann's picture of the Hanseatic merchant aristocracy of the nineteenth century, in his *Buddenbrooks*, and of the salons of the German bourgeoisie during the 1920s and '30s, in the latter parts of *Doktor Faustus*. One can think of many examples of remarkably convincing accounts of historical periods by the great novelists—Faulkner, Proust, Tolstoy.

However, having said all that, the distinction between history and fiction is profound. The literary imagination is boundless—and should be boundless. History is an imaginative construction, too; but the historical imagination must be bounded, closely bounded, by the documentation—limited by the evidence that has survived, and limited too by the obligation to be consistent with what has previously been established. It must somehow fit together with what is already known. While fiction can have an enormously stimulating effect on historical awareness, and novels can convey the quality of life in the past, the distinction between history and fiction is fundamental; and it is not diminished by the lack of total, absolute objectivity in what historians write.

The impossibility of writing history with perfect objectivity and the fact that historical writing is, in the end, an act of imagination are no new discoveries, and they do not mean that history is inevitably a form of free-floating self-expression—fiction by another name—and that any version one comes up with is as good as any other. As Robert Solow remarked in another connection, the fact that there is no such thing as perfect antisepsis does not mean that one might as well do brain surgery in a sewer. The correspondence to actuality in history, the struggle to describe objectively what actually happened, however dimly we may perceive it, is the essence of history. And that is so for everyone who writes a single page or paragraph or sentence of history, no matter what the technical epistemological problems may be—including those who write books (with admirable accuracy and objectivity) on the history of historians' failing efforts to attain objectivity.

Nothing is more certain to distort history by anachronism than making up direct discourse, fictional conversation, to put into the mouths of historical figures. And that is true no matter how skilled the historian is.

Samuel Eliot Morison, for example, the greatest American narrative historian since Parkman, slipped into fictional discourse repeatedly in his biography of Columbus, especially in describing the tense days and hours before the great discovery. He puts in the mouths of Columbus's sailors words like "keep her off, damn your eyes—must I go below and take the stick myself?" Or again: "Hear anything? Sounds like breakers to me —nothing but the bow wave you fool—I tell you we won't sight land till Saturday. . . . Here's a hundred maravedis says we raise it by daylight." I don't know how fifteenth-century Spanish and Portuguese sailors actually talked to each other, what their slang was, how they used ordinary street language, but these yo-heave-ho quotations sound to me like conversation one would have found in boys' adventure stories that students in St. Paul's School would have read early in the century— crossed perhaps with phrases Old Salts in Northeast Harbor, Maine, were supposed to have used. To me, it's not sailors of the fifteenth century that are made vivid in these fictional phrases, but a romantic twentieth-century historian straining for effect.

But you have also said that, for you, things really come together in "moments of creativity" when you are writing. How is that different from fictional writing?

⊙ B. B. ☺ I think it's very different. As I said before, no working historian, however philosophically sophisticated, can write a sentence of history without thinking that something in fact happened back there; that there was a real world back then, independent of our perception of it, and that, if the sources are available, one's job is to describe and analyze some aspect of that world. You have to assume that, and that assumption exerts—at least in a negative fashion—a control over what you can say. If it's history, it can be disproved. You can't disprove a novel, but you can disprove history; and that seems to me all the difference in the world.

Yes, there are wonderful "moments of creativity" in writing history, but they are not transcendental flights into the unknown. Creativity in science, the physicist Richard Feynman said, is imagination in a straitjacket. So, too, is creativity in history.

One of the most amusing approaches to this has to do with the now discontinued television series "Hill Street Blues." I once assigned a graduate seminar to watch that program for a while. At first they didn't get the point; they didn't see why as historians they should be watching it, especially since—and this *was* the point—they had a good deal of difficulty figuring out what was going on.

The people who made "Hill Street Blues" deliberately had four or five interrelated narratives proceeding simultaneously, and they pointed the camera straight into the turmoil of a chaotic police station. People were running this way and that; the stories kept getting interrupted, some never reached a satisfactory conclusion, seemed to remain open-ended; the characters spoke in code words peculiar to their own world; and sometimes you couldn't tell who was doing what. On top of all this, it was often hard to see who was right and who was wrong. Some of the most attractive characters did nasty things, and in some situations to do right would inevitably have bad consequences.

But isn't that what actually happens? Often, in one's own life, one doesn't know how things fit together or what will later prove to have been the major lines of development. In one's personal life there is a great deal of confusion; in a nation's or a society's life the confusion is enormous, apparently impenetrable. There are any number of narratives going on simultaneously; some will never be resolved, will simply be by-passed by other things and be forgotten; and good and bad will sometimes be difficult or impossible to separate.

In "Hill Street Blues" it was left to the viewer, to a surprising extent, to perceive the narrative structures and to form judgments. I thought that was a wonderfully realistic idea. Many people responded positively to the program's deliberate confusion, but some did not; and apparently the producers began simplifying it after a while—I suppose because too many people were confused, and they had their ratings to worry about.

Just so in history, it is left for the historian to sort out the narrative line, explain what moved together, what influenced what, what the stakes were in significant decisions, what the origins and consequences were. Historians are viewers, analysts, explicators of the hubbub of an infinitely confused station house, with people running in all directions, in a constant struggle for satisfactory solutions to their problems, their hopes and ambitions.

The fact that raw experience is confused, often bewildering, does not mean that clear historical analysis is false, only that historians seek, retrospectively, a clearer understanding than contemporaries could have had.

What distinction do you make between history and biography, both of which focus upon activity or subject matter of the past?

⊙ B.B. ⊚ There are areas in which biography and history are intermingled intimately. A good biography is a piece of history, but there are distinctions to be made—distinctions, I should say, suggested by Paul Lazarsfeld, a sociologist, when he was urged to write a memoir of his own career. He asked himself what possible justification there could be for doing this. He said in "An Episode in the History of Social Research"—and I think what he said relates as much to biography as to autobiography—that he could find only three reasons:

The first justification is if one is a person of great consequence in human affairs—Churchill or de Gaulle or Roosevelt; or a great figure in intellectual history, like Kant or Einstein. Any circumstance in such a person's biography is important, because we need every possible detail in order to understand what he or she did and why. If Napoleon hadn't had the temperament he had, if the details of his early life had been different, the world would be very different. Consequently, almost anything one can find out about the details and circumstances of Napoleon's life is important.

Second, Lazarsfeld said, an individual can be a representative of a group of some importance. He himself or she herself might not be important in the way that, say, Cæsar was; but as a representative of some sort or group of people, he or she might be very much worth studying in detail. In this sense, a relatively obscure person can very well justify an extensive biography that would be a contribution to history.

And, third, he concluded, some people are excellent witnesses. Although they may not have been representative of anything in particular and certainly did not shape history, they were present at the right place and the right time. Harold Nicholson, for example. He was a small man, not a very pleasant man in some ways, but he was near the center of things in the 1930s and '40s, and he recorded what he saw. His diary, published in abridged form in three volumes, is a fascinating witness to important events, especially as it captures the contingencies, the uncertainties, the false starts of the public events in his time and also the intersection of private and public events.

It seems to me that these are very good categories of biographies as history. For the rest, biographies are studies in human character, studies in human nature and in the fascination of people as such. Some people are strange, profound, amusing, evil, benevolent, intriguing, revealing—in all sorts of combinations. And one's under-standing of and interest in human nature are expanded by knowing about them—even such strange figures as Sir Edmund Backhouse.

Backhouse was an æsthete and accomplished sinolo-gist, who was also a pornographer and literary forger, who lived in an almost completely imaginary world. Somehow he managed to convince hard-headed men of affairs of his realism and practicality, passed himself off as the lover of China's Empress Dowager, and fooled al-most everyone with an apparently invaluable diary of the late-Manchu years, which he faked. He was a bizarre, gifted man. Trevor-Roper devoted a large book to him, and I read it with great interest, simply because Backhouse was so outrageous and interesting. However, that doesn't necessarily make good history, except as the historical background is drawn—in Backhouse's case, the story of late-Victorian æstheticism and the decay of the Manchu Empire.

Are there any observations that you might make about collaborative approaches to historical investigation and presentation—work pursued by two or more collabora-tors or by a historical "team"?

  ☙ B.B. ❧ Social scientists, like natural scientists, work in teams all the time, and authorship is often by many people. Physicists can list ten people or more as the authors of a given paper. Teams can sometimes work well in history, too—especially in technical, quantitative history. But I have not been able to do much of this myself. I have had assistants, and they have been a great help. One, with whom I have worked for many years, has become a kind of collaborator, but in the same way my wife was, in the computer study I mentioned before: by performing different functions from mine. In the end, it seems to me a historian has to resolve the issues into a personal statement and not a team statement.

I have collaborated in a full sense only once, with a very close friend and colleague, John Clive. We wrote an article together, on Scotland and America in the eighteenth century. He was in British history, I was in American history. We remained very close friends until his death in 1990—but not because of that collaboration. It was extremely painful. Not in working out the ideas; as soon as we talked about the cultural parallels between eighteenth-century Scotland and America, we saw the importance of their similar situations as provinces of metropolitan Britain, and we got up an outline with no trouble. The difficulty lay in the writing. Each of us had a certain pride in composition, and the result was almost a death struggle to get the phrases, the wording right, and to get the right balance between assertions and examples.

Collaborating like that requires a very intimate relationship, a close meshing of personalities—which is probably why some of the most successful collaborations have been of husbands and wives: the Webbs in Britain; here at home, the Beards, the Handlins, recently the Rutmans. But there have been others, too, whose collaboration seems to have melded two authors into a single identity: Robinson and Gallagher on the British empire in Africa, Fogel and Engerman on American slavery. The most common kind of collaborations in history, however, is found in the writing of textbooks. But that kind of collaboration usually means simply juxtaposing sections, on successive periods, written by period specialists.

Real collaboration is difficult because historical research is not a mechanical process that can be farmed out, piecemeal, to others and because, in the end, writing history is, as I said earlier, at least a craft—and at its best a form of art. Hence, it is the expression of individual skills and individual points of view.

To what extent do you, as a historian, find that what you write turns out to be rather different from what you thought your sources, initially or at an early stage, were saying?

☉ B.B. ☉ I find this happening all the time. I suppose there are some people who can think everything out in advance, and the writing is just a matter of expressing their thoughts. It isn't that way with me. After a great deal of study or research, I begin with what I believe is a clear and pretty detailed outline. But, then, it turns out that I think as I write. I see things I hadn't noticed before, and sometimes I become involved with the leading characters, who almost, as in writing a novel, take off on their own.

In writing the Hutchinson biography I found myself surprisingly sympathetic with this despised Tory governor, and I almost unconsciously began to play little tricks in composition to convey my own sympathy. I found myself dropping attributions; that is, I would start a paragraph saying, "Hutchinson thought . . . ," but for the next sentences down through the rest of the paragraph I didn't say that. I dropped the attribution, implying that it is I—that it is history—saying it, not Hutchinson; that, consequently, it is presumably true in a different sense than if it had simply been Hutchinson's view. I didn't set out to deceive anyone, but I simply assumed that the original attribution would carry through the paragraph.

One gets involved with characters or situations, and one's involvement can take over. You can get carried away. And that can lead to exaggeration. When I was working on *The Ideological Origins of the American Revolution* I suddenly saw anomalous things coming into focus. Mysteries kept cropping up, discrepancies I couldn't at first explain and which suddenly became clear. For example, the American pamphleteers talked frequently about Denmark. I couldn't figure out why on earth they were doing this. I knew they didn't know a thing, really, about Denmark—or about Sweden, which they also talked about. One had to track this down. It turned out there was a famous pamphlet of the 1690s called *The State of Denmark* by Viscount Molesworth. Obviously, Molesworth and this obscure business about Denmark were for some reason important to these people. I had to find out why, and did. In this way the pieces began to fall into place, one by one, until I could see the whole of the subject fairly clearly.

When one gets to that point it takes considerable restraint to keep from going overboard—from exaggerating the uniqueness and importance of what one had pieced together so carefully. The discoveries and the writing carry you along. When you've got new material that is really interesting, writing it out is thinking it through—and it does have its own impetus.

Have you ever, when writing, abandoned your original scheme of organization as you have progressed with your writing?

☉ B.B. ☉ I have frequently changed or expanded or contracted an original plan. My original outlines frequently fall to pieces or get elaborated into new shapes as I go along.

One teacher of freshman writing at Harvard, who liked *The Ideological Origins*, asked if I had any outlines or drafts of the chapters that she could show her students. I had kept most of the working papers, and I said that if she wanted to see them, I would bring them around. When I got to the class I realized that the boxes for each of the chapters were a mess—all sorts of scraps of paper, and an outline out of Rube Goldberg. I had begun with a very neat outline at the start, but then I kept appending pieces of paper, with scotch tape or staples. The original outline grew in every direction, with pieces hanging here and there. I gave it to the teacher, and she was quite disappointed with all these ribbons dangling down.

In this sense, I guess I'm not very well organized. But I don't apologize. I try to let the material shape the structure as far as possible. I remember in a seminar that I once took, the teacher, who was very well organized, said: "Now, you first get three-by-five cards which have a red line on top, this for the eventual bibliography. Then, you get five-by-seven cards for your notes— white for certain kinds of material, blue for other kinds. And, in the end, you put them, properly indexed, into boxes." I said to myself, if I ever teach a seminar, I'm going to go through that same routine, saying: "You get three-by-five cards; then, five-by-sevens that fit boxes nicely; and, then, you throw the whole thing out the window." I never quite did that, but it might have been a way to get students to work out their own procedures as they went along, and do what comes naturally. People have different styles, and each project has different technical requirements.

What is for you the relationship, in timing, between research and writing? How do you work that out?

☉ B. B. ☉ I haven't got any formula. There comes a point when you're deep enough in the material—can see the themes clearly and can control the information—and you feel the writing will go smoothly.

I've got masses of information on seventeenth-century social and demographic history, but it's only now beginning to come into focus—coming together into a configuration that has not been seen before, along lines of a controlling interpretative theme that I can outline in a preliminary way. Sometime soon I will know I can begin to write. There simply comes a time when the story begins to make enough sense, and one feels one can communicate it coherently.

One of the problems in all fields of scholarship is that of bringing projects or undertakings to a productive culmination. Do you have any observations or advice on this?

☉ B. B. ☉ It is a temperamental thing, I think—a matter of psychology. It seems to me that some people cannot live comfortably with unresolved tensions. They are uneasy if they have material prepared, projects started, but not finished. They seem to be impelled to resolve the tensions by finishing the projects. That gives them some relief.

I have sometimes exaggerated this in talking to graduate students—and created some alarm (until they know that I am, in a way, kidding)—when I've said that any good historian has to be a compulsive neurotic, in order to finish projects. There are some people, of course, who can live with unresolved and incomplete work.

But there is another element that enters into this, which is that if a project is not closed off at a certain point, it becomes boring; it drags and becomes stale; one loses interest, the impetus is gone; and one has to continue on mechanically, dissipating energy and becoming discouraged. One has to move along as quickly as possible or the thing may never get done.

Have you in your own work found things that you just did not want to complete and have not completed?

☙ B.B. ❧ Mainly what has happened is that projects that didn't get completed got shifted off into other kinds of things. For example, I had in mind once to do a very large-scale descriptive history of eighteenth-century politics. That got boiled down into *The Origins of American Politics*, a small book of three essays, entirely analytic. The masses of descriptive material I had accumulated were reduced to a separate section, set off from the rest by smaller typography. That highly condensed section, printed in a special typeface, is all that came of the large descriptive project. But the analytic book itself was based on my knowledge of the detailed narratives which I did not write. The intellectual substance, the importance of the narratives, had been drawn off into the little book.

Then, too, I set out many years ago to do a four-volume edition of the pamphlets of the Revolution. I did one big volume, and in the course of that made an intensive study of all of the pamphlets and wrote an elaborate introduction, which I called "The Transforming Radicalism of the American Revolution" and which became *The Ideological Origins of the American Revolution.* Having published all that, I found the other three volumes less compelling. But I have in mind—because I have just the kind of neurotic tendencies I mentioned before—to finish those three volumes, for which I have a great deal of new material prepared. (Part of the second volume has, in fact, been published separately.) I wasn't bored, but I had relieved the tension through writing out in this one book everything I knew about all of the pamphlets and associated material. Then, the mechanical task of editing the rest of the documents got put off.

What might you say about historical investigation and

interpretation as practiced within specialized academic or professional disciplines?

⊚ B.B. ⊚ I have been involved in that in one respect; namely, the history of education. In fact, my first university teaching was in the history of education, and I ended up writing a short book on the subject, *Education in the Forming of American Society.*

What I found, and wrote at the beginning of that book, was that professionals within a discipline, looking at the history of their discipline, get involved in severe anachronisms, because they seem impelled to search the past for the seeds, the antecedents, of the present, and they mistake cognates for real identities. Once you are involved in isolating from past contexts what you take to be antecedents of the present, you are foreshortening the past, because the past was different and those seeds, those cognates, had different meanings in earlier times. I tried to show how present professional involvements in education have distorted the history of education and have forfeited the history that can help one understand the contemporary situation. This greatly annoyed certain established people in the history of education, who criticized me severely for saying this.

The point is, that if what you are looking for are historical antecedents only—that is, the early little forms, the apparent rudiments—you are going to violate the context in which they existed, and very often you will misunderstand what the people were even talking about.

Take, for example, "public education"—public or free education, as we understand it. Public education and free education in the seventeenth and eighteenth centuries meant something quite different from what they mean now. When you spoke about "free" schools in the seventeenth century, it didn't mean that one did not have to pay fees. It meant that anyone of any religious denomination could enter it—free, in other words, to anyone who could pay the fees. It wasn't "free" in our sense. And "public," as you know from the present "public schools" of England, meant "private" in our present terminology.

In the history of medicine—and even more, I suspect, in the history of law—it seems to me you run the same danger of not seeing history whole, and, as in the history of education, one can distort the subject severely by anachronism. That is the danger of histories of the professions. But nowadays I think people are more aware of this problem, and they try to correct for it.

Would you cite a few individuals of the past, from within the field of history, whom you regard as among its most eminent practitioners—and tell why?

ⓒ B.B. ⓢ I did do this on one occasion and published it in a booklet called *History and the Creative Imagination.* I selected four historians who, it seemed to me, have had a peculiarly creative effect on historical understanding. By that I don't mean the most popular historians; they weren't particularly popular historians, but historians whose work shifted their subject substantially and irreversibly—so that it was never the same after they wrote—and gave rise to new ways of approaching a large area of the past. These were recent historians, scholars within our own present culture, who altered, enriched the basic understanding of large fields. And I tried to isolate the qualities and intellectual processes that lay behind their creativity.

What I found was, first of all, that each of them penetrated deeply into the context of past circumstances. They were all, deeply, contextualists. Second, they all were working with new data, masses of data that they had recently recovered or that had been known but that had never been used much before. And, third, all of them had some kind of personal involvement with their subject, which almost obliged them to think freshly and originally about it. One can trace the dawning of their perceptions and the ways in which large configurations grew out of their study of details.

I won't go through all of this, but let me illustrate one issue. One of the historians was Charles M. Andrews at Yale, who was a very important academic historian in his time, though now largely forgotten. He reconstructed for the first time the eighteenth-century Anglo-American administrative empire, showing the deep interconnections between the two peoples, and particularly the way early American public institutions grew from British origins. He did his main work, explaining and cataloguing and using masses of neglected documents in the Public Record Office in London, just before and during World War I, at a time when America's allegiances in the divisions of Europe were the subject of fundamental debate here in the United States.

Andrews was a Connecticut Yankee whose native culture was deeply Anglophile. He taught school in Hartford, Connecticut, for a while, and was at Yale during all of his career thereafter. His scholarship was meaningful to him in a personal way. He was able to show the age-old, almost immemorial connections between America and England, at a time when this was very much in question. While other historians affiliated with him were getting into this issue publicly, politically, and polemically (like George Louis Beer and others who were writing for *The Round Table*, the magazine of the empire, some of whom were even predicting that soon Britain and America would become politically reunified), Andrews never discussed political questions directly. But he did show in his history the deep historical affiliation between Britain and America, which must have satisfied him in some subjective, personal way.

So, too, the others I wrote about. Ronald Syme, for example, writing about the late Roman Republic and the Principate in a very rigorous fashion, using the elaborate genealogical data of prosopography, came to the conclusion that the development of politics in that period depended on recruitment of people from the provinces. New men came in from Spain and from elsewhere on the periphery of metropolitan Rome and joined the mainstream in Rome.

Syme was a New Zealander, who in time became the Camden Professor of Ancient History at Oxford. The whole process of moving in from the periphery, from the colonial provinces, somehow fitted him, and he worked the theme out broadly in a fascinating little book, *Colonial Elites: Rome, Spain, and the Americas*, in which he argued that the strength of empires frequently depended on recruiting or coopting the new aristocracies developing on the peripheries. I don't want to imply that this was mere self-expression on his part. His great book, *The Roman Revolution*, is highly technical history, but it is history that meant something personal to the author.

And, as I say, all of these historians—Andrews, Syme, and the others—were contextualists. All of them were working with new or freshly perceived data, just as all of them had some kind of personal involvement with the subjects they were explaining. Thus instigated, they began to see in the data connections of people and circumstances that had not been perceived before, and which together would form a new picture—one different from the previously familiar historical world.

🕭 B.B. 🕮 One was Perry Miller, who wrote on Puritanism in America. The personal side in his case is more complicated than with the others, but his analysis of his data—sermons that had been dismissed as theological rubbish—was as expert as Syme's prosopography or Andrews' administrative analyses.

The other was Lewis Namier, writing on eighteenth-century British history. Namier was a displaced Polish Jewish intellectual of a landed-gentry family. For him eighteenth-century England, as he viewed it, was profoundly satisfying. His arguments on the importance of secure landholding in eighteenth-century Britain and on what he took to be the non-ideological character of British politics (he hated ideas—or, rather, the belief that ideas shaped history) reflected his own biography, the losses and aspirations of his displaced, disoriented gentry family. In his biography, written by his wife, the deep emotional involvement he had with these technical questions of eighteenth-century British history becomes perfectly clear.

What is there to be said about the need or the appropriateness of writing history anew for succeeding generations?

🕭 B.B. 🕮 That relates, in a way, to what I was saying

about "definitiveness," because it seems to me that there is no end to the writing of history—nor should there be, because new questions come up and new techniques develop, new data are discovered, and succeeding generations will and should tell the story differently.

I mentioned Paul Lazarsfeld earlier. He had a peculiar interest in this question. He was much involved with survey analysis—that is, polling, questionnaires, and the mathematical techniques of analyzing the resulting data—and he published a paper in 1950 in which he asked: What does the pollster of 1950 owe to the historian of 1984?—in other words, what should contemporary data-gatherers, survey analysts, pollsters, collect for the use of future historians? It is an interesting paper, and I remember discussing it with him at length.

My view was, and is, that this is a misleading question, that one has no idea what a later historian will need or want to know. Lazarsfeld was sure one could anticipate what a future historian would want and that the pollsters of our own time could gather it. But though certain things, obvious things, can be anticipated, the more important things cannot be, since it is the subsequent development of our history that will create the more interesting questions. Of course, any background material is valuable, but one cannot make precise determinations of the data that will later be useful for historical questions.

But you ask about the appropriateness of writing history anew for succeeding generations. It must and will be done. Every generation will have its own approach and questions, since history is, in the end, an inquiry about the past. History is not an inert reconstruction of the past that gets set once and for all; it is a form of inquiry, and those inquiries will shift and renew and grow in time. Succeeding generations will write different kinds of histories—and should.

Graduate students entering the historical profession want to study and write about something new and original. But so much has already been done, it is today difficult to find a topic on which to concentrate. Did you experience this same situation when you yourself started out?

B.B. I was lucky enough to have some extraordinarily impressive historians as teachers. Their accomplishments seemed overwhelming and intimidating. But I was continuously struck by how different their interests were, not only from my interests, but from what most of my generation felt were exciting issues and problems—and also how different their terms of explanation were from what satisfied us.

Morison, for example, in addition to being a wonderful narrative historian, was an accomplished and devoted sailor, and in his lectures he would, in effect, sail the *Mayflower* into the harbor. We'd spend some time pulling on the halyards, so to speak; he would give us the sailing directions, explain the landfall, et cetera. But I wanted to know who these people were, what they thought they were doing, how they lived. Yet, the social history then being taught—which in its origins, in the "History of American Life" series, had been tremendously innovative—was highly descriptive, even enumerative (the dates of the first subways, the rise and fall of grain production, the expansion of frontiers, immigration figures, and the legislation on immigration)—very little of it analytic or explanatory.

As graduate students we did not think we were smarter than our teachers, but we had different interests, and we saw questions that didn't seem to concern them. Their most creative years had been in a different context, and they were not doing what really excited us. We wanted a fresh cut, exciting discoveries of our own.

Given the data that these very innovative historians had developed, one could do something analytically, we thought, that would be new. One had the feeling that the material they had assembled could now be used in subtler ways, more interesting ways. One had a sense of the possible expansion of their work into new areas. The question was whether one would have the chance—and, in the end, the ability—to do it.

Do you think that was an idiosyncratic reaction—something unique to your generation?

⟨ B.B. ⟩ No, but the burdens may be greater now. There are now over fifteen thousand members of the American Historical Association—about a third of them in American History. Almost all of them are professional scholars, and, as I said at the beginning of these conversations, they turn out a prodigious amount of material. That was not true in the years just after World War II. There just wasn't that degree of saturation, that much material, that many scholars at work, that number of periodicals and books being published.

The Harvard Guide to American History is an indication of this. It is a bibliography of American history. The first edition, in 1910, was a slim booklet, but it was reasonably complete. In 1954 Oscar Handlin edited the next version, and it was almost 700 pages of small type. The third edition, edited by Frank Freidel in 1974, is in two fat volumes—over 1,200 pages—and it just skims the surface. Now we don't know how to do a fourth edition, because of the size that a new comprehensive bibliography would have to be and the difficulty of deciding on the most useful principles of selection.

So, there is a quantitative difference. Still, despite all this, twenty years from now kinds of history will be published that we haven't yet thought of, things which our students will conceive, write, and publish that will supersede what we've managed to do. Historical writing has its history too.

⟨⟩———⟨⟩

Composition and printing
by The Stinehour Press

Design by the Editor